Artlist Collection
THE DOG

BEST IN SHOW

By The Dogs
As told to Apple Jordan

SCHOLASTIC INC.

New York   **Toronto**   **London**   **Auckland**   **Sydney**
Mexico City   **New Delhi**   **Hong Kong**   **Buenos Aires**

ISBN-13: 978-0-545-01184-6
ISBN-10: 0-545-01184-1

© 2008 artlist INTERNATIONAL

Published by Scholastic Inc. All rights reserved.
SCHOLASTIC and associated logos are trademarks and/or
registered trademarks or Scholastic Inc.

12 11 10 9 8 7 6 5 4   8 9 10 11 12/0

Printed in the U.S.A.
First printing, January 2008

Best in Show

Dogs make all different sounds, and we come in all different shapes, colors, and sizes, too. And each one of us has our own distinct personality. What makes one pooch howl may make another dog growl!

First of all, as much as we love our friends the mutts, dog shows are for purebreds only. But among the hundreds of different purebred dogs, there are standards that each dog must meet to be named "Best in Show" at competitive dog shows, according to the American Kennel Club. An extra pound or a drooped ear can automatically disqualify us from the competition. And you'd better not be in a grumpy mood that day. Biting the judge is a definite no-no!

Take a walk with us pooches, and we'll introduce you to some of the most popular purebreds around. As you'll see, we're each unique in our own way. But as much as we're different, we all have one thing in common . . . we need someone to love us!

Dog breeds are separated into the following groups:

- 🐾 Sporting
- 🐾 Hound
- 🐾 Working
- 🐾 Terrier
- 🐾 Toy
- 🐾 Nonsporting
- 🐾 Herding

Labrador Retriever

Doggy Data
Group: Sporting
Height: 21.5 to 24.5 inches
Weight: 55 to 80 pounds

Make no bones about it . . . we Labs are the most popular dogs on the block! And it's no wonder. We're playful, affectionate, friendly, and great with kids. Who wouldn't want us around?

Labradors come from way up north in Newfoundland, Canada, and were originally bred as retrieving dogs for hunters and fishermen. We fetched fish and helped swim nets to shore.

Labs need plenty of exercise. Being a couch puppy just isn't for us. Running and retrieving games are a lot more fun. But what we love best is a good swim. If there's a pool or lake nearby, be prepared to take a few doggy laps with us.

The only acceptable colors for a show dog Lab are solid black, yellow, or chocolate.

Yorkshire Terrier

Doggy Data
Group: Toy
Height: 8 to 9 inches
Weight: 7 pounds

We Yorkies might be some of the smallest dogs around, but we certainly don't think small. We love to play and are always up for some excitement . . . and sometimes a little mischief. If we're feeling feisty, we might even bark at a bigger dog. (But we hope he won't bark back!)

Yorkies come from across the "pond," all the way from Yorkshire, England. Our original job was to catch rats. Can you imagine? *Us* chasing rats? How un-Yorkie-like. Today we're usually spoiled by our human friends and never have to do a day's work.

Yorkies make great pets. For starters, our shiny coats don't shed. And we don't need a lot of exercise. A short romp is enough to keep us healthy. Furthermore, we're awfully cute! Who wouldn't want to spoil us and make us happy?

Dog Show No-No

Better ease up on those doggy biscuits! A Yorkie's weight cannot go above 7 pounds for competition.

German Shepherd

Doggy Data
Group: Herding
Height: 22 to 24 inches
Weight: 75 to 95 pounds

German Shepherds come in a variety of coat lengths and colors. But only our short-haired cousins with black-and-tan, black-and-gray, or all-black coats are show-dog material.

We Shepherds are smart, if we do say so ourselves. Because of our brains — not to mention our brawn — we're put to work on a number of important jobs, such as being guard dogs, police dogs, search-and-rescue dogs, and Seeing Eye dogs. And we take our canine responsibilities seriously.

But our most important job is to be a family pet: We're calm, loyal, protective, and brave. We're known to be a "one-man dog," devoted to the human friend who takes care of us best.

Golden Retriever

Doggy Data
Group: Sporting
Height: 21.5 to 24 inches
Weight: 55 to 75 pounds

Golden Retrievers have definitely earned the title of man's best friend. Doggone it . . . people like us! And why shouldn't they? We're faithful, friendly, gentle, and affectionate. We're great with kids, too. We have a high tolerance for tail tugging and horsey rides.

Our long, lush coats can be a deep golden color or a lighter cream color.

We Goldens were originally bred in England as retrieving dogs for hunters. We're strong athletes who need lots of exercise. That's easy for us to get because we love to run and play — we're always up for a good game of fetch. Today we're mainly family dogs, but some of us are trained as guide dogs for the blind. We help them get from place to place.

Dog Show No-No

We Goldies don't have a lot of wiggle room in the show-dog arena. If we measure just an inch above or below our standard height, it's an automatic disqualification. Male dogs should measure between 23 and 24 inches. Females should measure 21.5 to 22.5 inches.

Beagle

Doggy Data
Group: Hound
Height: 12 to 15 inches
Weight: 18 to 30 pounds

Dream Dogs
Unlike some of our sloppier friends, we Beagles don't drool.

Dog Show No-No

For competitions, a Beagle's tail shouldn't be too long. And any Beagle taller than 15 inches is automatically eliminated.

We Beagles have been around for a long time. In fact, we date as far back as 14th-century England, where we were used as scent dogs to hunt rabbits and other small game.

Beagles are some of the friendliest dogs around. We're independent and love exploring, but we're also playful and love our families. Because of our hound-dog instincts, we sometimes have a bad habit of wandering off. We like to follow a scent to wherever it might take us. So if you want to keep us in sight, you'd better put a leash on us!

There are two types of hound dogs: sight hounds, who hunt by chasing what they see, and scent hounds, who chase what they smell.

13

Dachshund

Doggy Data – Miniature

Group: Hound
Height: 5 to 6 inches
Weight: under 11 pounds

Doggy Data – Standard

Group: Hound
Height: 8 to 9 inches
Weight: 16 to 32 pounds

We funny little pooches were originally bred in Germany to hunt badgers. In fact, our name comes from the German words *dachs* (badger) and *hund* (dog). Because our low bodies are so close to the ground, we were able to chase badgers and foxes into their dens.

You can spot us Doxies easily—our long body, short legs, and crooked ears make us stand out from the crowd. We're playful pets who are devoted to our human companions. Although today we're mostly lapdogs, we still love to hunt and explore. We just follow our nose!

We Doxies come in two sizes — either miniature or standard — and three different types of coats: short-haired, long-haired, and wirehaired.

Dog Show No-No

Doxies are full of energy, so any show of shyness at competition time is definitely frowned upon.

 # Boxer

Doggy Data
Group: Working
Height: 21 to 25 inches
Weight: 50 to 80 pounds

Boxers come from Germany and are distant cousins of the Bulldog. We were one of the first dogs to be used as police dogs in Germany, probably because of our brawny physique.

Boxers are full of energy and need plenty of room to run. We may look a bit intimidating, but our bark is definitely worse than our bite. We have a playful personality that makes us the perfect family dog. We're great with kids *and* at guarding the house. And if our bark doesn't scare off intruders, our loud snoring just might!

Dog Show No-No

At competition time, a Boxer can't have white markings on more than a third of its coat.

Poodle

Doggy Data – Miniature

Group: Nonsporting
Height: 10 to 15 inches
Weight: 12 to 18 pounds

Doggy Data – Standard

Group: Nonsporting
Height: over 15 inches
Weight: 45 to 65 pounds

Don't hate us Poodles for being pretty . . . we're smart, too! In fact, the Standard Poodle is one of the smartest breeds around. We're easy to train, calm, and make good watchdogs. When you meet us, it will be puppy love at first sight.

Today the Poodle is the national dog of France, but we originally came from Germany. In fact, our name comes from the German word *pudel,* which means "to splash in water." No doubt we were given this name because we're such excellent swimmers.

Poodle show dogs require a lot of grooming to keep our fashionable fur looking perfect. But for non-show dogs, we don't mind our manes a little messy.

Dog Show No-No

All show Poodles have to be a solid color. No spots allowed!

Toy or Miniature Poodles were used for hunting a type of mushroom called truffles. But be sure to keep chocolate truffles out of sight. Chocolate is toxic to dogs and can make us sick!

Our fancy Poodle coat isn't just stylish, it's practical, too. Traditionally our coat was cut to make it easier for us to swim, but it was left longer on the chest to keep us warm. This style is still the standard look for Poodle show dogs today.

19

Shih Tzu

Doggy Data
Group: Toy
Height: 8 to 11 inches
Weight: 9 to 16 pounds

We Shih Tzus love to be spoiled. We're playful, affectionate, and sometimes don't mind being dolled up with a few ribbons and bows. But we're more than just a pretty face. We're smart and can be stubborn, too.

Dog Show No-No

Our coats shouldn't be thin or curly at competition time.

The Shih Tzu can be traced all the way back to ancient China. Our cute-and-adorableness has been captured in Chinese art dating as far back as 600 C.E. Our name means "little lion," but we've also been called "the chrysanthemum-faced dog" because of the funny way our hair grows all around our face. Whatever name you call us, we think "Best in Show" would be most suitable. Don't you agree?

Miniature Schnauzer

Doggy Data
Group: Terrier
Height: 12 to 14 inches
Weight: 13 to 15 pounds

Shnauze in German means "nose" or "snout," so our funny-sounding name refers to our long muzzle. (But we think it's impolite to call attention to one's more distinctive features.) Our hair grows wildly on our so-called schnauze, not to mention our eyebrows, mouth, and legs. Our wiry coats are either all-black, black with silver markings, or gray, also called "salt and pepper."

Miniature Schnauzers were originally bred in Germany as farm dogs used to catch rats. Yuck! Today we're better suited as family dogs and make playful and loyal companions to our human friends. Some of us Schnauzers like to bark a lot, so we make excellent watchdogs as well.

While we Mini Schnauzers are members of the terrier club, our larger cousins, the Giant and Standard Schnauzers, belong to the working dog group.

Chihuahua

Doggy Data
Group: Toy
Height: 5 to 9 inches
Weight: 2 to 6 pounds

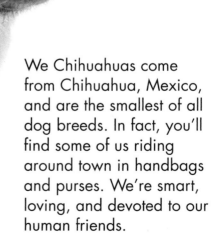

We Chihuahuas come from Chihuahua, Mexico, and are the smallest of all dog breeds. In fact, you'll find some of us riding around town in handbags and purses. We're smart, loving, and devoted to our human friends.

Dog Show No-No

A Chihuahua's tail should be full and long for competitions. A cropped tail gets us disqualified.

Despite our small size, we sometimes think we can run with the big boys. We might even challenge a larger dog if we're feeling spunky. But luckily, our human friends are always close by to scoop us up when trouble brews.

Chihuahuas can be a bit particular about who we spend our time with — we'd rather hang out with other Chihuahuas. After all, great company deserves each other, wouldn't you say?

All dogs — even the smallest Chihuahua — are descendants of wolves.

Bulldog

Doggy Data
Group: Nonsporting
Height: 12 to 15 inches
Weight: 40 to 50 pounds

Hot Dogs

We Bulldogs have a low tolerance for heat and humidity. It definitely makes our tails droop!

We Bulldogs were given the name "bull" because we originally were bred for bull baiting, a brutal sport that was popular a long time ago in England. We had to be vicious and tough. Fortunately, baiting was outlawed in 1835. Breeders then worked hard to rid the Bulldog breed of its more aggressive traits. And lucky for us, they succeeded!

Today, we Bulldogs are playful and friendly companions. We can be stubborn, too, but overall our gentle nature makes us the perfect pal to our human friends. You'd better buy a pair of earplugs if you want to spend a lot of time with us. Because of our flat muzzles, we're known to be heavy snorers!

Pug

Doggy Data
Group: Toy
Height: 10 to 11 inches
Weight: 14 to 18 pounds

With our flat faces, pug noses, and wrinkled-looking muzzles, we Pugs are hard to miss. We also have a funny little tail that curls and falls over one hip.

Dog Show No-No

The show Pug's tail should be tightly curled. A double-curled tail is even better.

Pugs are the largest of the toy breeds, and we're also one of the oldest dog breeds around. We date all the way back to 400 B.C.E. China! We lived in Tibetan Buddhist monasteries, and later made our way to Europe where we hobnobbed with royalty. We were favorites of kings and queens. And why wouldn't we be? Our human friends love us because we're playful, friendly — and oh so adorable!

More Top Dogs!

Rottweiler

Pomeranian

Maltese

Boston Terrier

Cocker Spaniel

Bassett Hound

Shetland Sheepdog

Doberman Pinschers

Welsh Corgi

Miniature Pinscher

And the winner is . . .

As you can see, no two dog breeds are exactly alike. We each have our own history, temperament, personality, and style. But every one of us is filled with lots of love and affection for our human friends! This makes us all worthy of a "Best in Show" award, don't you think?